MIGUEL MAÑARA

MIGUEL MAÑARA

by Oscar Vladislas Milosz

With a commentary by
Luigi Giussani

HAB
HUMAN ADVENTURE BOOKS
TAMPA

Miguel Mañara
By Oscar Vladislas Milosz

Translated by from the French by Edo Morlin-Visconti

Translation and introduction to the play used by kind
permission of the translator.

Commentary by Luigi Giussani property of The
Fraternity of Communion and Liberation. Used with
permission.

Original title:
Miguel Mañara. Mystère en six tableaux (1913)
In the Public Domain

CONTENTS

LUIGI GIUSSANI

Commentary on
MIGUEL MAÑARA

From a reading of the play with a group of
university students in January, 1980

I'd like to read some selections from Miguel Mañara by Milosz. It is, together with Paul Claudel's The Announcement to Mary one of the texts that helped to build the beginning of our movement's history. At that time, these texts were practically memorized by all of us.

Miguel Mañara is the real Don Giovanni, a true historical figure in the mid-sixteen hundreds. He is the Spanish Don Giovanni who gave rise to all the subsequent Don Giovanni characters later invented. He is rich in all senses; in all the talents and possibilities imaginable and, therefore, is hopelessly arrogant. Everything is owed to him, and everything must serve his pleasure and his opinion. Violence, in the most subtle and masked sense, is his law of life. The knights of the king's court respect him as "the best." He's much younger, not more than half the age of the others.

At the beginning of the play, at a party given in his honor, there is a dialogue in which they provoke him to remember all his bold adventures, especially all his adventures with women; women of any type and social class. He answers their requests, however, at the climax of the admiration hailed on him by the others who cry out: "Glory to Mañara, glory to Mañara in the depths of hell," Miguel suddenly says:

I am pleased to see, sirs, that you all love me a lot, and I am deeply moved by the heartfelt wish you express of seeing my flesh and my spirit burning alive in a new flame, very far from here. I swear before you on my honor and on the head of the Bishop of Rome that your hell does not exist, and has never burned except in the mind of a mad Messiah or of an evil monk.

But we know that in God's empty space there are worlds illumined by a joy warmer than ours, unexplored and wonderful lands that are very, very far from this one. So, go ahead and choose one of these far and delightful planets, and send me there, this very night, through the grave's greedy door. For time passes slowly, sirs, terribly slowly, and I am strangely tired of this bitch of a life. Not to reach God is certainly a tiny thing, but to lose Satan is a great sorrow and a huge bore, by my faith!

I have drawn Love into pleasure, into the mud, and into death; I have been a traitor, a blasphemer, an executioner; I have done all that a poor devil of a man can do, and look! I have lost Satan. I eat the bitter herb of the rock of boredom; I have served Venus angrily, then maliciously, and disgustedly. Today I would yawn as I twisted her neck. And it is not vanity speaking through my mouth. I do not pose as an insensitive executioner. I've suffered; I've suffered a lot. Anguish has winked his eye at me; jealousy has whispered into my ear, pity has grabbed me by the throat. Really, these were the least deceptive among my pleasures.

So! My confession takes you by surprise; I hear some of you laughing. Know then that there is no-one who ever committed a truly shameful action who did not cry over his victim. Certainly in my young years, I too sought, just as you do, the miserable joy, the restless stranger who gives you her life without telling you her name. But the desire was soon born in me to pursue what you'll never know: a love immense, dark and sweet. More than once I thought I had caught it, and it was only a ghostly flame. I'd embrace it, with an oath I'd promise it eternal tenderness, it would burn my lips and cover my head with my own ashes, and when I'd open my eyes again, there was only the horrible day of loneliness, the long, endless day of loneliness, with a poor heart in its hands, a poor, poor sweet heart, as light as a sparrow in winter. And one evening, the vile-eyed and low-browed lust came to sit on my bed, and looked at me in silence, as if looking at a dead man.

Do you know what I need, sirs? A new beauty, a new sorrow, a new love that I'll soon be fed up with in order to taste better the wine of a new evil, a new life, an infinity of new lives. That's what I need, sirs, nothing else.

Ah, how do I fill up this emptiness in life? What can I do? For the desire is always there, stronger and madder than ever. It's like a fire in the sea that blasts its flame into the deep universal black emptiness.

It is a desire to embrace the infinite possibilities. Ah sirs, what are we doing here? What do we gain? Ah, how short is this life according to science! And, as for weapons, this poor world wouldn't have enough to satisfy the appetites of a lord like me; and as far as good works are concerned, you know what troublesome dogs, what a stinking brood of rats men are; and certainly you know too that a King is a very poor thing once God has gone away.

There's no difference between this cry of Miguel Mañara and this other great sentence of Gide: "Desire, I dragged you through the streets, I dissipated you in the fields, I got you drunk in the city, I got you drunk without quenching the thirst, I got you wet in moonlit nights, I brought you around everywhere, I rocked you on the waves, I wanted to make you fall asleep on the water. Desire, desire, what have I done to you? What, then, do you want? When will you tire out?"

Among those present, there's the eldest, the only wise and well-balanced man in the group, a friend of Miguel's father. He had an intuition that the thirty-something son of his friend was going through a horrible and desperate moment. He has a picture in his mind of Miguel in the house of another of his friends who had only one daughter, very young, an intelligent, beautiful, direct, serene woman.

The second scene gives the dialogue, the first in depth dialogue between Miguel and Girolama, which is a presence, the Presence: "Why", says Miguel, "have I never realized before that I have a good soul?" It is a presence, in fact, that makes possible the awareness of himself. What has this deep, calm, free, pure adventure of love become in the life of Miguel? What has it become in the life of each of us here?

The whole dialogue, which should be read again, word by word, intense and great is it, tells the story of the event of this change for Miguel.

DON MIGUEL

You love flowers, Girolama? And I don't see them in your hair or on your person.

GIROLAMA

It is because I love flowers that I do not like girls who adorn themselves with them, as with silk or lace or colorful feathers. I never put flowers in my hair (it's beautiful enough, thank God!) Flowers are beautiful living beings that we must let live and breathe the air of the sun and of the moon. I never pick flowers. We can very well love, in this world where we are, without wanting immediately to kill the one we love, or to imprison it behind glass, or, as people do with birds, to lock them up in a cage in which water no longer tastes like water and summer seeds no longer taste like seeds.

DON MIGUEL

So everything is honey, and dew, and balm of sweetness in you, Girolama? Is there no dark corner in your heart? Do you never get angry?

GIROLAMA

But yes, yes! And even against these flowers, I like so much, because their Latin names are so hard to remember. They have earned me an infinite number of lectures from our abbot, who, instead of contenting himself with being a good geometrician, dedicates himself to botany, too, to my great misfortune.

You were telling me awhile ago that my life was sad; I don't agree at all. There is the house, there is the garden, the daily lesson, and there are the poor. There are many, a great many poor people in Seville. I have no time to get bored. And then there are books. You see, I am the one who reads to my father. I know almost all our poets, and recently we acquired "The Adventures of the Illustrious Knight of La Mancha". My father and the abbot laughed a lot, and I wanted to cry. How beautiful are the books that make you laugh and cry at the same time!

But maybe I am stretching your patience too long, Don Miguel, and you must be judging me very dull and garrulous. You look a bit surprised at seeing me so happy. Do not reproach me for this peace of mind and heart, for I neglect none of my duties.

DON MIGUEL

I was the one, Girolama, who asked you to tell me the story of your dear life. Oh sweet life, oh beautiful and sad flower! Do not withdraw your hand; leave it here on my heart. Let the beating of my heart manage to tell you what I don't dare entrust to my voice. I've so many things to tell you! I am so changed from the day we met! It was at the church of Caridad, remember? Around Palm Sunday, before I left for Madrid; and that same evening Don Fernando, your father's old friend, pushed me by the shoulders into this house which I feared, because you knew my life, you knew of my life what can be revealed to a young girl, and it is a lot, I'm afraid, it is too much, Girolama.

GIROLAMA

I spoke to Don Fernando, maybe I should not confess these things to you, I spoke to Don Fernando about you. I'm no longer a child and I think that nothing is better than beautiful frankness. And Don Fernando spoke to me about you. You know how he is, our old friend Don Fernando: a bit of a teaser, but a good fellow. He pulled my leg (he knew me as a baby), then suddenly he changed his tone, and even his expression. And he spoke to me about you.

DON MIGUEL

Alas, Girolama! There is no remedy to this sadness of the heart! What's done is done. Because life is like that. What's done is done.

GIROLAMA

I don't agree in the least. I see nothing so terrible in this. I know you are a bad lot, who has made many ladies cry, and beautiful ones, too. But all these women knew they were doing wrong in loving you, and even in allowing you to love them. For you have given none of them the oath, the great oath that binds for eternity, Don Miguel; and you had given none of them the ring, the ring that unites soul to soul forever, Don Miguel. Ah, they knew very well what they were doing, all of them, yes, all of them!

DON MIGUEL

Silence! Your voice frightens me, Girolama! It is as if a summer-beam suddenly penetrated into a place protected by the wings of night, full of crawling shapes, of things dreamt of by the sickness of darkness. One day I saw a Sister of Mercy pushing her way all alone into the cell of those condemned to death. This how your voice advances, Girolama, into my evil heart.

GIROLAMA

It is because you take me for a stupid little girl; it is because you don't know me well, Don Miguel. And also, it is because I am small and weak, and I am sure you feel a great compassion for me, fearing you could break my wing or my little paw. But I give you leave to speak to me freely. I am not afraid of you. Something in my heart tells me I'm your sister, I am not afraid of your eyes. No, Miguel, your look does not frighten me. I know well that at times, you are watching me as one watches a small animal he wants to catch, and it always makes me laugh when I think of it. You say woman is weak; all men say it, I think, for my father says it, and the abbot says it, and Don Fernando. And books say so, too. It's a fact, woman is weak, but like the bird in the air and the small mouse in the fields: it is not enough just to want to in order to catch it. And women know very well what they are doing, come off it, and don't let themselves be taken except when God is no longer in their heart, and then it's no longer worth while taking them. I know well what I say and do, otherwise, would I have come here, alone? I took great interest in letting you know me, Don Miguel. For you, I know you. Three months have passed since the day we met (at Caridad, Don Miguel); and you certainly were not then as you are now.

DON MIGUEL

Yes, Girolama, what you say is true; I am not what I was. I see better: yet I was not blind; perhaps it was the light that was missing; for the exterior light is a small thing; it is not the one that enlightens our life. You have lit a lamp in my heart; and here I am, like the sick man who falls asleep in darkness with the embers of fever on his forehead and the ice of desertion in his heart, and who suddenly wakes up in a beautiful room in which everything is immersed in the discreet music of light; and he sees the friend he has mourned for many years…a friend who saves him from the flood of darkness! Behold what a place of peace you've changed my heart into, Girolama! My sweetest sister! For, a while ago you said you were my sister, didn't you?

GIROLAMA

You are the man saved from the flood of darkness, and you are weak and pale and still stupefied, and it is well and necessary that a sister should think for you and speak for you and support you on the way, and should pray to God for you. Aren't you the man saved from the bitter water? And then, certainly I am your sister.

DON MIGUEL

But if you truly are my sweet sister, Girolama, precisely my... No, I cannot say it, my voice is no longer my voice, my heart is no longer my heart, my life is no longer my life... Girolama, give me your weak hand, your dearest hand of a friend, of a sister, of a holy spouse!

GIROLAMA

Are you talking to a young girl or to a woman? Beware, for heaven is listening, Don Miguel.

DON MIGUEL

I am talking to a woman under the shining sky of my joy, under the heavens suspended above our heads like a perfumed vault. I am talking to you, Girolama! Who are very great, so very great as to make me afraid? What have I done with my life, what have I done with my heart? Why didn't I learn earlier that I have a good soul? Will you forgive me?

GIROLAMA

I will have to forgive you. Get up.

DON MIGUEL

What about your hand?

GIROLAMA

I will have to give it to you.

DON MIGUEL

What about your heart? Are you going to refuse it to my joy? Tell me, what about your heart?

GIROLAMA

My heart is no longer mine.

17

DON MIGUEL

And your great purity, and your own holiness, will you entrust them to me, for as long as Time, for as long as Life lasts?

GIROLAMA

For as long as Eternity.

DON MIGUEL

And do you love me? Do you love me with a devoted love before men?

GIROLAMA

Before God.

The tones of the drama do not diminish the truth of this upright presence of one to the other. It's a rebirth: "That there not be remedy for this sadness of heart! What is done is done. Because that is what our life is like: what is done is done," Miguel said at a certain point in the dialogue. And Girolama counters: "I don't share at all this way of thinking of yours." There is a Presence because of whom the past, with all its evil, becomes a life, a different life, becomes the truth of the very existence that was ignored before: "Why didn't I realize before that I have a good soul?"

And it's like a recovery of the world, like someone who

exits the night for the first time and sees, finally sees. An embrace of everything becomes possible, an embrace of what was distant, of what was lost, of what was near but he didn't see it, an embrace of family, of dogs. What Girolama is a sign of to Miguel is a presence that makes you embrace, that raises up in a universal embrace. These factors belong to the structure of our life. A little or a lot, each of us has had a foretaste of these things as a nearness. If we are here it is because of this kind of encounter. However distant an echo it might have been, this is the kind of Event that has engaged me. Indeed, what is each of us for the other if not this companionship that cherishes and cares for [us] like an intention of the heart? What are we doing here? What do each of you mean for the other? When one day you find yourselves, man and woman, together, and it is to your advantage to continue on together, will it be for a solely human attachment, yet without echoes, without perspectives, without voice? But what are you for her, and you, what is he for you? If you do not aspire, if you do not freely allow your heart to journey toward the ideal, to walk toward this different life, then what are you if not a lump in which the other, botching up, seeks a response to his instinctivity or to his state of soul?

At a certain point, Girolama said, "One can indeed love, in the world we live in, without having suffered the desire to murder one's beloved" or without having desired to grab in order to possess, in order to stop; rather than give him a hand in the journey towards destiny, one murders and puts an end to him.

After three months of marriage, Girolama unexpectedly dies.

So Miguel finds himself virtually suspended over a vertiginous abyss within which he no longer has support, no longer has a presence. And he cannot go back to the way he was before, because once you have glimpsed certain things, you cannot return to the way it was before. The presence is no longer there, but what that presence gave him a presentiment of remains. He can no longer deny that truth of the world, that perspective on his journey, life's destiny. But where can it be found? So, desperate, a seeker of support, of companionship, of a presence, he knocks at the door of the Convent.

The fourth scene of the drama is the dialogue between Miguel and the Abbot, in whose character is revealed another aspect, another form, of the same companionship. The core of the dialogue in this scene lies in the impetuous unveiling of what prayer is. Here is the possibility of companionship that, in any moment and condition of life whatsoever, makes man sense the presence that cannot fail, a possibility that makes man sense all the precariousness and limit of human presence, which is a sign of this Presence with a capital P.

In Girolama, a fragile woman who dies, or in the powerful figure of the Abbot, who is limited by the great rule, prevented from accompanying him step by step, even the limit of human companionship, which is a sign of that Companionship, becomes a part of him and does not vanish, no longer withdraws. Thus the sign becomes ever more powerful, the more it might seem to slip away. Don Miguel makes his confession, crying out in despair over himself and his life, dominated by shame for his evil. The presence of Girolama, the absence of

Girolama makes all the vomit of his past life return.

THE ABBOT

Come on, come on, do not cry, my son. No! He does not want to smile, my begging monk. I cannot get a smile out of him! Don't you understand then, my son? The fact is you are thinking of things that are no more (and that never were, my son).

But is it necessary to repeat to you that you have come, that you are here, that all is well? What is there in that head of his, Lord?

DON MIGUEL

How can you read my heart in this way, Father? You did not even give me time to open it all to you. How do you read my heart, a closed book, like this, Father?

THE ABBOT

Get up. This way you have a strange air. And stop embracing my knees. Can't you keep quiet? I'll have your cell prepared. Do you hear me? I want to have you very close. Your nights will be very long, deserted, and hard; just wait a bit, man dressed in vanity! You are going to find out what it's all about, and you are going to know how a man prays, alone, at night, between four walls of eternity. Ah, it is not your fountains of tears under the moon, these prayers among four walls that pretend to be deaf, these litanies virgin of thought and naked of reason, and as long as the shadow of love that escapes. I want to have you very close. But you will never call for me. Understand? You will only say to yourself, the Father is there, behind these walls that never dream. The Father is there, he is old, and he sleeps on his three planks. And I, I am all alone with the heart of stone, and I breathe my prayers into the ear of stone. For you men dressed with colors say that walls have ears for your plots and your blasphemies. But here, where life is a thing very different from a smile in the lipstick or a woman's tear fallen on glass, here the stones are full of a patience that waits and a waiting that listens.

DON MIGUEL

Dark cell! Image of my heart! Lovable mortifications! Silence of catacombs! How I love you already!

THE ABBOT

Love and haste do not agree, Mañara. It is by patience that love is measured. A pace both regular and sure: this is the pace of love, that walks between two jasmine hedges, arm in arm with a girl, or alone between two rows of tombs. Patience. You have not come here, sir, to be tortured. Life is long here. Infancy and education are needed, youth and teaching, a maturity curious about the right weight of things, and a slow old age in love with the grave. With what prudence must we move then! For the burning hair-shirt has no love for the violence that quenches the blood's itching, and you must keep very still in a short, narrow coffin, when you huddle in it with the sound desire to sleep an hour or two in a sleep as empty and as deep as the instant.

To let your own blood is something sweetly fiendish; and sleeplessness consumes the heart. Now, life is long here, you understand. And too exasperated a hunger is a temptation. You must chew the foul grass and the lukewarm root like an animal which has before it beautiful meadows and long, long hours of summer.

And you must talk to Eternity with precious and clear syllables even at night, when its love grabs you by the throat like a murderer.

Know too that it is an excellent thing to remain faithful to the word that was ordered, a dam of granite for the bitter waters of your love! For it is necessary that prayer be a fast before it is a banquet, and nakedness of heart before it is a mantle of heaven buzzing with worlds. Perhaps a day will come when God allows you to enter brutally, like an axe, into the flesh of the tree, and to fall madly like a stone, into the night of the water, and to slip, singing like fire, into the heart of metal.

He adds: "All that might well happen someday, when the serpent, my dear child, has shed his skin," that is to say, when the perception of God and of Christ have become nearly transparent in the plant and in the tree and in the water, when the mystery that is the core of the plant, of the water and of metal, of the earth and sky, when the mystery

23

that is the heart of everything is no longer separated, as if the veil had fallen, like when you see the outline traced by the body that is behind the veil.

All this can well come one day, dear son, when the snake has changed his skin. But one must start from the beginning: this is essential. To bite the stone and to bark: Lord, Lord, Lord! Is to serve, weeping, a heartless woman. You must leave this to the betrayed who sigh a night, or six months, or ten years.

Life is long here.

You will beware therefore of inventing prayers. You will sing humbly with the book of the poor in spirit. And you will wait.

From the last nightly spark of your madness, the first dawn will spring up!

The crater of the heart cries and thunders and the black vomit will leave the cloud, then fall back in grey famine on the field and the vineyard. The prayer that devastates passion is like that. But when the heart has fallen asleep in the balm of the years, when the flesh has died and the blood has gone pale and when the marrow has gone dry, and when love is past and when sorrow is past, when love and sorrow and hatred have become ghosts that the sword penetrates as it does water and in which the lip hits nothing more than its own wound, as in molten glass, it is then that you speak to God no longer of yourself and of your own miserable unhappiness, but of man, and of the foam, and of the sand, and of the wind and the rain! Do you know which saint said, Behold brother wind and sister rain?

O my son, if you knew what things man can tell God when man's flesh becomes a cry, the cry of God worshipping Himself!

You do not have the face of a man who is listening, Miguel. You are thinking too much of your own sorrow. Why do you seek sorrow? Why are you afraid of losing what has managed to find you? Penance is not sorrow. It is love.

And the abbot leaves the scene. Now Mañara is alone and from these things, after a long life in the convent, the final soliloquy begins.

DON MIGUEL

Look at the moon, look at the earth, look at man so weak and at his great sorrow. And yet, despite all these things that are, I dare not say that You are.

Who am I then that I should dare say that You are? I am not sure, I have no right to be sure of anything apart from one: of my love, of my love, of my blind love for You. Nothing is pure, except my love for You, nothing is great, except my love for You. The dream has vanished; the passion has run away, the remembrance was cancelled. Love has remained. Nothing is sincere, except my love for You; nothing is real, except my love for You, nothing is immortal, except my love for You.

For I am nothing but one dead man among the dead

whom I have loved, I am nothing but a name that fills the mouth of the living with sand. What's left is Love. Ah, Beauty! the sad, poor Beauty! But I want to praise Beauty, for it is from it that Sorrow is born, the beloved of the Beloved. Your great love burns my heart, your great love my sole certainty. O tears! O hunger for eternity! O joy! Alas! Forgive! Alas! Love me!

There are great men and small men, there are mature men and there are children, but the story line of humanity, the story line of the heart is in the mature man as it is in the child. We are children, but we are called for this journey, where nothing is lost, nothing is forgotten, and, above all, nothing is renounced. On the contrary, everything is regained, everything is finally found. From the appearance of beauty, the sadness that redeems it comes about and, finally, love comes about, because the word "to love" has no chance whatsoever of being ambiguous; it is to affirm with wonder, with the wonder of all one's being, the Other, Destiny, and this presence of Destiny, this sign, this body of destiny that is other men and the sky and the earth and everything that happens. My goodness, my sorrow and my evil become worthy of love. Everything is new. "Everything is new," says Saint Paul. Behold, the old has passed away, it no longer exists. We are children. Why, this is the path we are called to, before everything. There's nothing to forget or renounce, there's no mutilation. There is only a resurrection.

We are not afraid, even though the appearance is mortification. What is mortification? It is what lies within what Christ Jesus' relatives said in the Gospel: "Come home, you're mad." Indeed, even though everything evidently corresponds to the awaiting of our heart, corresponds passionately, indisputably, we're dealing with an announcement that is totally foreign to everyday speech and to everyone's speech. Yet we are called to become great like this.

Let us pray to the Lord, pray to Him who has given us Being, the Father, He who is our destiny, original consistency of our life and our end; let us pray to He through whom we are born in every instant, that He make of our lives such a mature fruit, that He make us so great, that He make us run the whole length of the journey. Let us pray, let us ask God.

Prayer, let's remember, is asking Christ and that's it. Because within that there's father, mother, brother, sister, husband, wife, boyfriend, girlfriend, friend, companion, man, sky, and earth. It's there within. This, indeed, is the formula of the truth: "God, all in all." It's the formula of existence towards the explosion of that truth: "Christ, everything in everyone," that is, the Mystery of our companionship, the fragile and precarious but true sign of his Presence. Let us pray to God.

MIGUEL MAÑARA

Oscar V. Milosz

MIGUEL MAÑARA

Oscar V. Milosz
Introduction

THE AUTHOR

Oscar Vladislas Milosz was born in 1877 in Lithuania, and died in Fontainebleau, France, in 1939.

His father, Vladislas Milosz, had married Marie Rosalie Rosenthale, a Jewess, and kept her away from any social life, because Jews were the objects of spite in the Lithuanian milieu. During his early years, the poet suffered a lot because his mother was always full of resentment towards her husband and even mistreated the child.

In 1889, the family moved to Paris, and the father sent Oscar to a French High School. From this moment, the heart of Milosz was divided between a strong, nostalgic affection for his Country of origin, Lithuania, and its Catholic culture, and the charm of the French language and the secular education he received at school. His poetry and dramas will be written in French, but many of his publications will draw from the well of his remembrances of the cold forests and wintry songs of his beloved Lithuania.

From 1899, he wrote and published various books of poetry. In 1910, he wrote a novel, The initiation to love, which bears the signs of his conversion, and in which he affirms that "He who truly loves, loves God". From 1911 to 1915, he wrote most of his dramas, among which Miguel Manara, Saul of Tarsus, and Mefiboseth are outstanding.

When in 1918 Lithuania became an independent Republic, he obtained citizenship and immediately joined the Diplomatic Service, representing his Country in France as Charge d'Affaires. In 1925 he resigned, but remained attached to the Embassy til 1938, when he abandoned all diplomatic activity, one year before his death.

During these years, he spent much energy making the culture and tradition of Lithuania known to the French public and to Western Europe in general. He also wrote philosophical and mystical works. His last publication, in 1938, by the title The ky to the Apocalypse, presents his studies on the interpretation of the Bible.

MIGUEL MAÑARA

This drama is defined by the Author a "Mystery in six Flashes", where each "Flash" is a scene circumscribed, a story within the story, the locus where man has a unique, unrepeatable encounter with the Mystery of God.

Miguel Mañara tells the story of the conversion of a Spanish nobleman of the 17th century, don Miguel Manara, from the career of an exceptional womanizer to the highest degree of holiness.

The first Flash shows how bored a man can become in a life dedicated to sin, despite the unequalled success his peers accord him. We could call this Flash the description of the first insurgence of Religious Sense in a person. There always comes a point, the Author seems to say, where long-repressed fundamental questions can no longer be dodged.

The second Flash presents to us the story of a resolutive encounter. Don Miguel is introduced to a young girl, Girolama who strikes him because she is different from all the others he has met before. The veteran womanizer is captured by her gentle firmness and by her deep attachment to prayer, and realizes he cannot establish with her the kind of relationship he is used to: he cannot "use and dispose of" Girolama. Fascinated by her humanity, so different and fresh, he learns to pray again, and eventually asks her to marry him in Church.

But Girolama dies three months after the wedding. In the third Flash, the young widower recognizes in his sorrow the way in which God is calling him to a new life, a life containing on earth the seed of eternity.

He seeks refuge and spiritual solace in the Convent of Caridad. The fourth Flash displays his encounter with the Father Superior. The Abbot receives his confession and invites him to join the Carmelitan Religious life as his only chance to undergo a real change. The long nights in prayerful penance will enable don Miguel, he promises, to fully experience the love of God, after a life spent in debauchery and in the profanation of love.

In the fifth Flash, the Author exposes us to the visible signs of God's fruits in a man who has really entrusted his own life to His hands. Two religious men talk to each other about Friar Miguel's astonishing conversion. A man who truly is changed by God's love can become an instrument of His loving power: through Miguel, a lame beggar is miraculously healed in the public square.

The sixth Flash shows the apotheosis of conversion. A very old Friar Miguel dies and is welcomed by the Father in heaven in the way that had been prophesied to him many years before. To those who love God and are chosen by Him to enter His Mystery present on earth, maturity is indeed the coming true of the dreams of youth.

Edo Morlin-Visconti

Dramatis Personae

Don Miguel Mañara Vincentelo De Leca

Don Fernando

Don Jaime

Don Alfonso

The Abbot of the Convent of Caridad at Seville

Two Religious Men of the same Order

Johannes Mendelez, a Paralysed Beggar

Gorolama Carillo De Mendoza

The Shadow

The Spirits of the Earth

The Spirit of Heaven

Voices from the crowd

The scene opens at Seville, in the year of grace 1656

FIRST FLASH

The castle of Don Jaime in the countryside of Seville. A banquet in a brightly lit hall. Almost all the guests are already the worse for wine.

Don Jaime, a short plump old man of brutish appearance, is standing on a chair reproaching waiters and valets with a raucous voice.

DON JAIME

By the wounds of Christ! It seems to me that my guest, Don Miguel Vincentelo de Leca, knight of Calatrava, is letting himself die of thirst! God forbid that I should force you, Lenten-faced rogues, to stuff yourselves with black meat or yellow fat, or to drown yourselves in wine. We are, if our Lord Bacchus does not induce me into error, in the holiest of the yearly seasons, between Ash Wednesday and Palm Sunday. So then, rascals, fast, by all the devils, till the Catholic fast pushes through your skin with all its long rotten teeth, that are nothing but your own son-of-a-bitch bones; but, by Mohammed, go on serving as in the ordinary reveling and boozing time; or else I will send you to fast till Judgments Day in the antechamber of Monsignor the Archbishop, that saintly arch-miser. Come on, some wine, some wine! Or else, hell, I am going to swear in such a way that you will all be damned.

37

Wine is brought

And then if the Inquisition appears in the doorway, draw your swords, you lazy rascals, draw your swords and ready with the fuses, by the devil! Because...

DON MIGUEL

Sit down, you damned bawler, and stop bragging. Who here does not know your madman's antiphon! Here's one who thinks himself an enemy of Christ, yet, on my honour, would never dare, on a Good Friday, to lay hands on a scullery-maid caught in the dark passage between the cellar and the kitchen.

DON JAMIE

Ah, villain, come here onto my heart! Let me give you a great smacking kiss! You can teach the rest of us! What are we, poor miserable-looking devils, what are we compared to you? But what am I saying, compared with your shadow! You really are what I can call a wicked bastard. Look how handsome he is tonight! Eleanor, Blanche, Lawrence, and you Ines, and Cynthia, and all of you down there, just look at him! Have you ever set your eyes, you bitches, on a nobler forehead, a more beautiful mouth, a more passionate eye? And this silky lace from Venice, this shirt, by Bacchus! This king of shirts! And this sword, and this dress! Tell me, son, how many duchesses have you got on your conscience?

MANY VOICES

Yes, yes! How many seated duchesses? How many duchesses with the right of stool?

DON MIGUEL

Six.

DON JAIME

How many high-ranking marquesses?

DON MIGUEL

Seven, eight, or nine, if my lord Eros does not deceive me.

DON JAIME

And noble and middle-class girls?

DON MIGUEL

Between sixty and a hundred. I don't keep a full list.

DON JAIME

And small-time whores?

DON MIGUEL

There was once one who loved me truly, and died of unfeigned despair.

Short silence

And she died, sirs, almost at the same time as Sister Magdalene of the Compassion, stolen from Jesus thanks to my attentions.

ALL

Glory to Mañara, glory to Mañara in the lowest of hells!

Tumult of laughter, shouts, tinkling of silver and clinking of glasses.

DON MIGUEL

I am pleased to see, sirs, that you all love me a lot, and I am deeply moved by the heartfelt wish you express of seeing my flesh and my spirit burning alive in a new flame, very far from here. I swear before you on my honour and on the head of the Bishop of Rome that your hell does not exist, and has never burned except in the mind of a mad Messiah or of an evil monk. But we know that in God's empty space there are worlds illumined by a joy warmer than ours, unexplored and wonderful lands that are very, very far from this one. So, go ahead and choose one of these far and delightful planets, and send me there, this very night, through the grave's greedy door. For time passes slowly, sirs, terribly slowly, and I am strangely tired of this bitch of a life. Not to reach God is certainly a tiny thing, but to lose Satan is a great sorrow and a huge bore, by my faith!

I have drawn Love into pleasure, into the mud, and into death; I have been a traitor, a blasphemer, an executioner; I have done all that a poor devil of a man can do, and look! I have lost Satan. I eat the bitter herb of the rock of boredom; I have served Venus angrily, then maliciously, and disgustedly. Today I would yawn as I twisted her neck. And it is not vanity speaking through my mouth. I do not pose as an insensitive executioner. I've suffered; I've suffered a lot. Anguish has winked his eye at me; jealousy has whispered into my ear, pity has grabbed me by the throat. Really, these were the least deceptive among my pleasures.

So! My confession takes you by surprise; I hear some of you laughing. Know then that there is no-one who ever committed a truly shameful action who did not cry over his victim. Certainly in my young years, I too sought, just as you do, the miserable joy, the restless stranger who gives you her life without telling you her name. But the desire was soon born in me to pursue what you'll never know: a love immense, dark and sweet. More than once I thought I had caught it, and it was only a ghostly flame. I'd embrace it, with an oath I'd promise it eternal tenderness, it would burn my lips and cover my head with my own ashes, and when I'd open my eyes again, there was only the horrible day of loneliness, the long, endless day of loneliness, with a poor heart in its hands, a poor, poor sweet heart, as light as a sparrow in winter. And one evening, the vile-eyed and low-browed lust came to sit on my bed, and looked at me in silence, as if looking at a dead man.

Do you know what I need, sirs? A new beauty, a new

sorrow, a new love that I'll soon be fed up with in order to taste better the wine of a new evil, a new life, an infinity of new lives. That's what I need, sirs, nothing else.

Ah, how do I fill up this emptiness in life? What can I do? For the desire is always there, stronger and madder than ever. It sis like a fire in the sea that blasts its flame into the deep universal black emptiness.

It is a desire to embrace the infinite possibilities. Ah sirs, what are we doing here? What do we gain? Ah, how short is this life according to science! And, as for weapons, this poor world wouldn't have enough to satisfy the appetites of a lord like me; and as far as good works are concerned, you know what troublesome dogs, what a stinking brood of rats men are; and certainly you know too that a King is a very poor thing once God has gone away.

in a low voice, turning to MIGUEL

DON ALFONSO

If you see me here despite my white hair, Miguel, it is because I have been keeping an eye on you for a long time.I used to be the best friend of your father, Don Tomaso Vincentelo de Leca; and I knew your mother, Donna Girolama Anfriano. Your mother was a holy woman. Your father was a worthy man, faithful to God and his King. He died in my arms. Look at me, Miguel. You see I do not lower my eyes and I am no paler than before because I tell you what I must: you are a coward and a criminal

DON MIGUEL

Are you mad or drunk, Don Fernando, or are you tired of living?

DON FERNANDO

You know I have grown old in very holy battles, and that I will never part from my sword, even in death. I have had four horses killed under me, and I speak to the king face to face without taking my hat off. I could pull your ears, you scoundrel, but I content myself by repeating: you are a coward and a criminal. Whoever mistreats a woman and betrays her is a coward and a criminal. And who ever desires the woman of another man is a vile bastard. And who ever robs the least country girl of the holy treasure of her virginity, and then abandons her to her shame and despair, whoever does this is a dog, and must die like a dog. You are no gentleman, Miguel, you are a dog. Your coat-of-arms is something to be pinned above the door of a brothel. Is it my fault if the smell of your face-powder and of your make-up reminds me of a dog's smell? Tell me, Don Miguel, knight of Calatrava, is it my fault? If your father were alive, I would spit in your face; but your father is dead. He is no longer here to defend the honour of his blood; and your mother is no longer here to dry the cheek of her child and to console him in her arms.

What have we come to? Is this today's chivalry?

Even a Jew in the stench of his ghetto, a Jew faithful to his wife and tender with his little ones is a thousand times more of a gentleman than yourself! For whom then did we fight, powers of heaven! For whom then did our King sacrifice his own life, he who could not even love according to his heart, he who went pale and yellow before time in the dust of the State parchments. Alas!

He hides his face between his hands.

A rather long silence

DON FERNANDO CONTINUES

Listen to me, Miguel. You are young. Thirty years old. I don't know if I should laugh or cry! You are blessed with a nasty but powerful reason. Thirty! It's like the smell of grain fields, like the smile of night at the window where a face must appear, sweetly illumined by the heart of a rose.

Miguel! My son! My child! I am a crazy old man! I have talked to you like an old idiot! I have been unjust. When I was young, I liked girls, too. I didn't seduce them, I didn't take them for a ride, I did not abandon them, but I liked them, I desired them. I have been young too, Miguel. Forgive me. Forgive this rough old soldier. I am no man of the Court; I am not versed in courtly language. Good heavens! We have had a hard life! You must not be angry with me! You must forgive me. You are handsome, Miguel, you have a high brow, and bold eyes. Give me your hand. Come on, give me your hand.

A short silence. He considers Don Miguel's hand

It is a noble hand. The fingers are slender, the veins are light blue, a light blue that is so hard to find these days. And you are like your father.

Long silence

Listen, Miguel. In Seville, our good old town is a modest and very ancient house, not far from the church of Caridad. The house belongs to a very old gentleman. Your father knew him. I am his friend from childhood. His name is Carillo de Mendoza. He is sick and a widower for four or five years.

Short silence

This Carillo de Mendoza, my dear son, has only a daughter to console him in his suffering. The name of this girl, his only daughter is Girolama. It is your mother's name, Miguel. So this girl's name is Gorolama Carillo de Mendoza. She is a noble girl. She is a very nice and good and beautiful. She is just out of her childhood. You are thirty, Miguel. Oh, if only I were thirty! But you are the son of my friend and I forgive your being thirty. You never go to church, you rascal? You will go to church next week, Miguel. We'll meet there, if you like. Come, son, come. It is at the church of Caridad.

Don Fernando walks out. Silence.Almost all guests have left the banquet hall. Some have fallen asleep in the armchairs or under the table. There are some short candle stumps dying out; one can feel dawn is approaching. A Shadow pulls aside a curtain and appears to Don Miguel.

THE SHADOW

Blessed is the man whose heart is like a tombstone under the snow and whose hope is like the name of a father inscribed in the tombstone.

Blessed the man whose belly is the place where the cross is planted and whose blood is like the fear of the dumb.

Blessed the man who is cursed by his blind mother. She lifts her stick under the moon. The heart of silence is slashed to pieces.

Blessed the man whose tears are the rains of the ruined gravestones, and whose skin is the noise of the snake among the leaves.

Blessed the man whose son is begotten by the lust of the enemy! His son follows him in the silence of the snow, hiding behind the trees, and the cold moon looks on.

But woe, woe to the conscious man who, blind to God's beauty, prefers the emptiness of boredom to the torment of passion, and the torments of passion to the emptiness of boredom!

DON MIGUEL

Who are you Spirit?

THE SHADOW

I am the shadow of your past life.

SECOND FLASH

Garden of Seville in front of the house of Carillo de Mendoza

GIROLAMA CARILLO

I was not yet twelve, Miguel, when she died. It will be four years around St. John's Day in December. It is so good to die like that, with a pure heart and a clear mind, it is so good that at times I reproach myself for having cried so much. But then I was only a weak child, and certainly my little orphan tears did not offend God. Because we are very young at twelve. I know girls of that age who are still children. Afterwards I reflected so much. My father was already sick. You have known Don Clemente Carillo only a short time, but you have already been able to see that he is a bit moody, and sometimes harsh because of such a long sickness. It is a terrible thing to be condemned to immobility. Especially for a gentleman accustomed to the life of arms.

DON MIGUEL

And how come, Girolama, I never meet young girls of your age in this silent house? You seem to lead a very sad life, Girolama!

GIROLAMA

I have no friends of my own age, Don Miguel, and to tell the truth, I easily do without the company of girls of my own age. You see I don't like either the way they laugh nor the way they cry. And sometimes they talk among themselves about men in a way I don't like to hear talk about men and the love of men. Yes, we lead a very retired life. In winter, I don't leave the house except to go to church; but in summer we spend Sundays in the country. It is one hour from Seville. We have a house there with a big, big garden, and I love flowers very, very much.

DON MIGUEL

You love flowers, Girolama? And I don't see them in your hair or on your person.

GIROLAMA

It is because I love flowers that I do not like girls who adorn themselves with them, as with silk or lace or colourful feathers. I never put flowers in my hair its beautiful enough, thank God!Flowers are beautiful living beings that we must let live and breathe the air of the sun and of the moon. I never pick flowers. We can very well love, in this world where we are, without wanting immediately to kill the one we love, or to imprison it behind glass, or, as people do with birds, to lock them up in a cage in which water no longer tastes like water and summer seeds no longer taste like seeds.

DON MIGUEL

So everything is honey, and dew, and balm of sweetness in you, Girolama? Is there no dark corner in your heart? Do you never get angry?

GIROLAMA

But yes, yes! And even against these flowers, I like so much, because their Latin names are so hard to remember. They have earned me an infinite number of lectures from our abbot, who, instead of contenting himself with being a good geometrician, dedicates himself to botany, too, to my great misfortune.

You were telling me awhile ago that my life was sad; I don't agree at all. There is the house, there is the garden, the daily lesson, and there are the poor. There are many, a great many poor people in Seville. I have no time to get bored. And then there are books. You see, I am the one who reads to my father. I know almost all our poets, and recently we acquired " The Adventures of the Illustrious Knight of La Mancha". My father and the abbot laughed a lot, and I wanted to cry. How beautiful are the books that make you laugh and cry at the same time!

But maybe I am stretching your patience too long, Don Miguel, and you must be judging me very dull and garrulous. You look a bit surprised at seeing me so happy. Do not reproach me for this peace of mind and heart, for I neglect none of my duties.

DON MIGUEL

I was the one, Girolama, who asked you to tell me the story of your dear life. Oh sweet life, oh beautiful and sad flower! Do not withdraw your hand; leave it here on my heart. Let the beating of my heart manage to tell you what I don't dare entrust to my voice. I've so many things to tell you! I am so changed from the day we met! It was at the church of Caridad, remember? Around Palm Sunday, before I left for Madrid; and that same evening Don Fernando, your father's old friend, pushed me by the shoulders into this house which I feared, because you knew my life, you knew of my life what can be revealed to a young girl, and it is a lot, I'm afraid, it is too much, Girolama.

GIROLAMA

I spoke to Don Fernando, maybe I should not confess these things to you, I spoke to Don Fernando about you. I'm no longer a child and I think that nothing is better than beautiful frankness. And Don Fernando spoke to me about you. You know how he is, our old friend Don Fernando: a bit of a teaser, but a good fellow. He pulled my leg he knew me as a baby, then suddenly he changed his tune, and even his expression. And he spoke to me about you.

DON MIGUEL

Alas, Girolama! There is no remedy to this sadness of the heart! What's done is done. Because life is like that. What's done is done.

GIROLAMA

I don't agree in the least. I see nothing so terrible in this.
I know you are a bad lot, who has made many ladies cry,
and beautiful ones, too. But all these women knew they
were doing wrong in loving you, and even in allowing you
to love them. For you have given none of them the oath,
the great oath that binds for eternity, Don Miguel; and you
had given none of them the ring, the ring that unites soul to
soul forever, Don Miguel. Ah, they knew very well what
they were doing, all of them, yes, all of them!

DON MIGUEL

Silence! Your voice frightens me, Girolama! It is as if a
summer-beam suddenly penetrated into a place protected
by the wings of night, full of crawling shapes, of things
dreamt of by the sickness of darkness. One day I saw a
Sister of Mercy pushing her way all alone into the cell of
those condemned to death. This how your voice advances,
Girolama, into my evil heart.

GIROLAMA

It is because you take me for a stupid little girl; it is
because you don't know me well, Don Miguel. And also,
it is because I am small and weak, and I am sure you feel
a great compassion for me, fearing you could break my
wing or my little paw. But I give you leave to speak to me
freely. I am not afraid of you.

Something in my heart tells me I'm your sister, I am not
afraid of your eyes. No, Miguel, your look does not frighten

me. I know well that at times, you are watching me as one watches a small animal he wants to catch, and it always makes me laugh when I think of it. You say woman is weak; all men say it, I think, for my father says it, and the abbot says it, and Don Fernando. And books say so, too. It's a fact, woman is weak, but like the bird in the air and the small mouse in the fields: it is not enough just to want to in order to catch it. And women know very well what they are doing, come off it, and don't let themselves be taken except when God is no longer in their heart, and then its no longer worth while taking them. I know well what I say and do, otherwise, would I have come here, alone? I took great interest in letting you know me, Don Miguel. For you, I know you. Three months have passed since the day we met at Caridad, Don Miguel; and you certainly were not then as you are now.

DON MIGUEL

Yes, Girolama, what you say is true; I am not what I was. I see better: yet I was not blind; perhaps it was the light that was missing; for the exterior light is a small thing; it is not the one that enlightens our life. You have lit a lamp in my heart; and here I am, like the sick man who falls asleep in darkness with the embers of fever on his forehead and the ice of desertion in his heart, and who suddenly wakes up in a beautiful room in which everything is immersed in the descreet music of light; and he sees the friend he has mourned for many hears, the friend returned from overseas standing there smiling at him with eyes that are calmer and wiser than before, and there is the whole family, the old men with their white hair and the children

52

dressed brightly as ripened wheat, and there is the huge old dog, with its round eyes full of a tender laughter, and mouth open wide and full of happy noises to feast he man who was saved from the flood of darkness! Behold what a place of peace you've changed my heart into, Girolama! My sweetest sister! For a while ago, you said you are my sister, didn't you?

GIROLAMA

You are the man saved from the flood of darkness, and you are weak and pale and still stupefied, and it is well and necessary that a sister should think for you and speak for you and support you on the way, and should pray to God for you. Aren't you the man saved from the bitter water? And then, certainly I am your sister.

DON MIGUEL

But if you truly are my sweet sister, Girolama, precisely my... No, I cannot say it, my voice is no longer my voice, my heart is no longer my heart, my life is no longer my life... Girolama, give me your weak hand, your dearest hand of a friend, of a sister, of a holy spouse!

GIROLAMA

Are you talking to a young girl or to a woman? Beware, for heaven is listening, Don Miguel.

DON MIGUEL

I am talking to a woman under the shining sky of my joy, under the heavens suspended above our heads like a perfumed vault. I am talking to you, Girolama!, who are very great, so very great as to make me afraid. What have I done with my life, what have I done with my heart? Why didn't I learn earlier that I have a good soul? Will you forgive me?

GIROLAMA

I will have to forgive you. Get up.

DON MIGUEL

What about your hand?

GIROLAMA

I will have to give it to you.

DON MIGUEL

What about your heart? Are you going to refuse it to my joy? Tell me, what about your heart?

GIROLAMA

My heart is no longer mine.

DON MIGUEL

And your great purity, and your own holiness, will you entrust them to me, for as long as Time, for as long as Life lasts?

GIROLAMA

For as long as Eternity.

DON MIGUEL

And do you love me? Do you love me with a devoted love before men, before men?

GIROLAMA

Before God.

THIRD FLASH

Three months later. A room in Don Miguel Manara's
palace at Seville. Girolama Carillo lies on a narrow,
white bed without flowers. Four candles burn, immobile.
Don Miguel is crouched in a dark corner of the room.
The Spirits of the Earth.

FIRST SPIRIT

Her eyelids are tightly closed, her jaws are firmly locked;
her arms are crossed on her breast and her hands are joined
around a small wooden cross, as hard as bone. Her head
rests on a pillow, neither too high nor too low, the robe
does not show any crease the robe is a perfect fit, the feet
touch each other lightly. I am satisfied with my work.

SECOND SPIRIT

They have brought the coffin; I have seen it. It is of pure
silver, but two strong men can life it easily, because it is
practically the coffin of a child.

THIRD SPIRIT

They have opened the old crypt of the Vincentelo de Lecas.
It's in perfect order. Two or three bricks to be replaced,
two strokes of a trowel, and everything is in place.

FIRST SPIRIT

Tomorrow towards midday, brothers, we have to go to the house of old Carillo Mendoza. As he heard of the death of his only daughter, the poor man fell into the arms of his old friend Don Fernando, with out a cry, without a tear, after which he never opened his mouth again, and tomorrow is the third day.

DON MIGUEL

Good people don't make this noise of words, I pray. Do what you need to do in silence, please. I do not reproach you men for your work, but stop discussing my dear one among yourselves. I know she is dead, but I do not want people to speak of her as of a dead person.

FIRST SPIRIT

He takes us for men made, like he is, out of clay and tears. And it is his great love that reads like this into the closed book of thoughts.

SECOND SPIRIT

His sad thoughts are like voices of unknown men in a dark and frozen house.

THIRD SPIRIT

There is no need to pity him. Man belongs to the earth. He has to worship the Spirit of the Earth.

To Don Miguel

Man of clay, tears have drowned your miserable brain. Saltless words drop on your mouth like lukewarm water. Wake up, look! You are alone.

DON MIGUEL

If it is my madness hat speaks, if it is truly the voice of my madness that I hear, thanks be to you, O Lord my God. Let Madness take my head on her knees and sing in my ear: my little one, my little one! I do not want to be cradled by a girl. The arms of girls are as cold as death. And do not tell her, my friends that I am weeping: this would tear her poor heart to pieces.

THIRD SPIRIT

Get up, speak and act, and weep like a man, Aren't you a man, Mañara? Aren't you a son of Sorrow?

Get up; the mourning clothes are ready. You must walk up to the grave with a dignified air. And watch out for the mud on the road, for it is already autumn. Three months have elapsed since the summer day of your wedding. You must not overlook the calculation of the months and the days, son of the Earth?

DON MIGUEL

I will follow the coffin as a small child that is led to the church; and I will do all that they'll tell me to do. I am a poor unhappy man. I do not want people to get angry because of me. And I will not go and hang myself among the willows by the riverside. I will do nothing that God forbids. God has created me, and I will have to go on living.

THIRD SPIRIT

Think of the Earth, son of Sorrow. All the rest is worth nothing. You have a heart for hope, and hands for work. You need to go on living, and to live long, and to say with men: It is a joy for me. And when your arms will be broken, and when your old bones will pain you, and when your white hair will be like the disease of the tree, one day youwill get up earlier than usual and you will light the frail lamp in the grey hour, and you'll set your hand to work for the last time.

FIRST SPIRIT

But on the threshold like a barkless branch you'll fall. Then the big cold bed will be opened.

SECOND SPIRIT

And the coffin will be brought.

THIRD SPIRIT

And the crypt of the Vincentelo de Lecas will be opened.

THE THREE SPIRITS

But till that beautiful day you must live, son of Earth.

*The Spirits go away. A long silence. The hours are heard
to strike.*

DON MIGUEL

Sorrow, Sorrow, why did you beget me? Why did you not crash m head between two innocent stones, more kind than the breasts of your love?

You tell me, Sorrow, that you are my mother. But if you are, you must know what hell cries here, mother, in this old hear. Is it for this you lulled me in the winter nights, in the light of fireplaces, where orphaned time cried out? Tell me: is it for this that you lulled me with tears and dreams in your sad eyes, in your dear eyes the colour of journey and of wind? You laid me in a cradle: would that you had thrown me in to a grave! You kissed my body from the small feet to the poor head: why weren't you like the beasts in the woods, who choke their cubs to death, O mother!

Cursed be your sweetness, you who gave me birth in sorrow! Cursed be your belly, cursed be your womb, you who gave me this sad body, this lonely heart?

And yet you are not the sister of the she-wolf who gives birth hungry in the light of a sad moon like a face kissed by the plague. We must leave tenderness to the females in the woods, whose skin tastes of hunger: aren't you the daughter of men, O Sorrow?

Mother, Mother, I have lost everything, my life is widowed,

my lust weeps and I am the father of fright, of folly, and of death. O Sorrow, my mother, what did you make of me?

THE SPIRIT OF HEAVEN

Mañara, Mañara!

DON MIGUEL

Who is calling me? I know this voice. Where did I hear it before, and when? It is as if the echo of birth-cry should be awakened suddenly in an old man's heart.

THE SPIRIT OF HEAVEN

Mañara, Mañara, beloved son!

DON MIGUEL

It is like the ghost of a sweet sun on the water, it is like the steamy breeze of the apple-tree.

THE SPIRIT OF HEAVEN

Mañara, Mañara, rejoice!

DON MIGUEL

I do not understand you. Speak more clearly.

THE SPIRIT OF HEAVEN

Open your ear.

A short silence. Under the windows there passes a procession.

SONG

The sweat of death runs on his eyes. He walks under the cross towards his last day,. What thing of beauty is there here to be seen, tell us, son of Man?

The water of this country is like the eye of the blind man, the stone of this country is like the heart of the King, the tree of this country is a torture pole of you, Love, son of Heavens.

He has broken the bread, he has poured the wine.

This is the flesh, this is the blood.

Let he who has ears hear!

He prayed and got up: his beloved ones were lying under the olive tree.

Simon, are you asleep?

He cried and he got up: his dear children were dreaming under the olive tree. You can sleep now, says the son of Man. They came with swords and lanterns: "I greet you, Master". The brother has kissed the brother on the cheek. The right ear was cut, and see, it is healed: so that man may understand.

The cock has crowed twice: there is no love left, all is forgotten.

The cock has crowed in the loneliness of your hear, son of Man.

The crown is on your head; the reed is in your hand, the face is blind to the spit and the blood.

Hail, king of the Jews.

The clothes have been divide, the thieves are dead.

"I thirst", the heart of life cries out.

But the sponge has fallen back and the side is pierced and all is accomplished.

Now we know that he is the Son of the living God and that he is with us till the end of the world. Amen.

DON MIGUEL

Amen.

FOURTH FLASH

Parlour of the Convent of Caridad, Seville

DON MIGUEL

Father, here am I asking for asylum. And for protection.

THE ABBOT

And against whom, my son?

DON MIGUEL

Against myself.

THE ABBOT

Who are you then?

DON MIGUEL

Mañara.

THE ABBOT

Taking one step back

Your place is not here. You have the smell of burning about you.

DON MIGUEL

It is the Eternal love that consumes me, Father.
He throws himself on his knees.

THE ABBOT

And what do you come here to seek, my son?

DON MIGUEL

The punishment of the jealous God; humility of heart; love for reality.

THE ABBOT

You talk like a poor sinner. Get up. I know your crimes, Don Miguel de Leca; but it is necessary that the black confession pour from your mouth like the ugliness of vomit. The repentance of the heart is nothing if it doesn't climb all the way up to the teeth and if it doesn't flood the lips with bitterness. If you are God's friend, then, speak. And it is necessary that the Truth be naked, without any veil of shame or sorrow. Say: I did this, I that. Speak.

DON MIGUEL

I did not work the six days. I have done no work at all. And on the seventh day, my work was to blasphemy, to spit on the earth and on God. I honoured neither father nor mother. My father cursed me, my mother died of sorrow.

I lied. A thousand times, I said: I said I love, while my heart was laughing a wicked laughter. And a liar can take back what he has said but I, how could I take back what I have said?

I stole. I stole innocence. But the penitent gives back, and I, I cannot give back.

I killed. And my victims are black with my sin before the face of God and filthy with their lust, my own. I have desired the house of my neighbour; I even set the house of my neighbour on the fire with my desire. And it is a house that one cannot rebuild with money. I did all this. I did all this, Father.

Silence

And then a woman stood up at the bend of the bad road. She was calm like the dream of water, beautiful like the light of honey, innocent like the laughter of small children. She talked to me of God, and taught me to pray. At night, I repeated the words of her prayer, like a child. The woman's name is Girolama, Father. Girolama Carillo Mendoza is the name of my wife, Father.

THE ABBOT

The love of this woman, of this Girolama, was a very good thing. Why then are you here, and all tears, Don Miguel Mañara?

DON MIGUEL

This woman, all sweet and all mine, this Girolama, Father, is dead.

THE ABBOT

Come on. Weep if you need to, but do not make all this noise.

He prays for a moment, then he lifts up his face

DON MIGUEL

I haven't told you everything, Father.

THE ABBOT

One must not talk again of these poor things, of these stupid things, my grown-up child, do you understand? These are stories to be left to those whom the great pride of the small sins still torments.

But you Miguel, my great villain, beloved son, what can you have to tell me? Who does not know the great Manara? For a long time I've been watching you. We see everything here, in spite of our eyes on the breviary. Listen to me. I've let you cry on my lap, and you cried like a new-born. And now I lift my finger, and see how full of anger I am, and listen to how I shout: Silence! What do you know of your sorrow, my son? You came here to be reproached and scolded, and know you are reproaching Penance for its sweet voice. They are all the same; they are terrible, these children. Since the lord is sweet, they would like to stuff themselves till they burst. You had come out of your house as if you were going to buy fruit. You have come. You are here. And all is well.

DON MIGUEL

I am afraid of your great compassion, Father. I feel so wrapped up, embraced by kindness. You must not be so sweet, Father. I feel I'm melted by your dear tenderness. I am ashamed. Nobody had ever spoken to me like this.

THE ABBOT

But yes, but yes.

You have been much loved, and you know it very well, you rascal, because they talked sweetly to you many many times. Are you going to be ungrateful? No. You say so because you are dressed in vanity, because your hair is clean and well combed, because you wear a beautiful jacket thank God I am not a young girl!, and your white hands have clean and well-cared-for fingers. You would like, I bet, to be already dressed in rags, waving around a long grey beard still with dirt and heavy with rain and letting the smelly cobblestones resound with your penitent's bowl, my graceful dandy.

Come on, come on, don't cry, my son. No! He does not want to smile, my begging monk. I can't smile out of him! Don't you understand then, my son? The fact is you are thinking of things that are no more and that never were, my son.

But is it necessary to repeat to you that you have come, that you are here, that all is well? What is there in that head of his, Lord?

DON MIGUEL

How can you read my heart in this way, Father? You did not even give me time to open it all to you. How do you read my heart, a closed book, like this, Father?

THE ABBOT

Get up. This way you have a strange air. And stop embracing my knees. Can't you keep quiet? I'll have your cell prepared. Do you hear me? I want to have you very close. Your nights will be very long, deserted, and hard; just wait a bit, man dressed in vanity! You are going to find out what it's all about, and you are going to know how a man prays, alone, at night, among four walls of eternity. Ah, it is not your fountains of tears under the moo, these prayers among four walls that pretend to be deaf, these litanies virgin of thought and naked of reason, and as long as the shadow of love that escapes, I want to have you very close. But you will never call for me, understand? You'll only say to yourself, the Father is there, behind these walls that never dream. The Father is there, he is old, and he sleeps on his three planks. And I, I am all alone with the heart of stone, and I breathe my prayers into the ear of stone. For you men dressed with colours say that walls have ears for you plots and your blasphemies. But here, where life is a thing very different from a smile in the lipstick or a woman's tear fallen on glass, here the stones are full of a patience that waits and of a wait that listens.

DON MIGUEL

Dark cell! Image of my heart! Lovable mortications!
Silence of catacombs! How I love you already!

THE ABBOT

Love and haste do not agree, Mañara. It is by patience that
love is measured. A pace both regular and sure: this is the
pace of love, that walks between two jasmine hedges, arm
in arm with a girl, or alone between two rows of tombs.
Patience. You have not come here, sir, to be tortured. Life
is long here. Infancy and education are needed, youth
and teaching, a maturity curious about the right weight
of things, and a slow old age in love with the grave. With
what prudence must we move then! For the burning hair-
shirt has no love for the violence that quenches the blood's
itching, and you must keep very still in a short, narrow
coffin, when you huddle in it with the sound desire to
sleep an hour or two in a sleep as empty and as deep as
the instant.

To let your own blood is something sweetly fiendish;
and sleeplessness consumes the heart. Now, life is long
here, you understand? And too exasperated a hunger
is a temptation. You must chew the foul grass and the
lukewarm root like an animal which has before it beautiful
meadows and long, long hours of summer.

And you must talk to Eternity with precious and clear
syllables even at night, when its love grabs you by the
throat like a murderer.

Know too that it is an excellent thing to stick by the word
that was ordered, a dam of granite for there at bitter waters

of your love! For it is necessary that prayer be a fast before it is a banquet, and nakedness of heart before it is a mantle of heaven buzzing with worlds. Perhaps a day will come when God allows you to enter brutally, like an axe, into the flesh of the tree, and to fall madly like a stone, into the night of the water, and to slip, singing like fire, into the heart of mental And that day you will know of what flesh the world is made, and you will speak freely to the soul of the world of the Tree, of he Water, and of the Metal, and you will speak to it with the voice of the wind and of the rain and of a woman in love.

My son! Man has cried numberless times, not prostrated, but standing up straight before God, breathing his love onto him full in His face, like a fire in a forest or in a great city, and the Lord laughed, because the angels were afraid. All this can well come one day, dear son, when the snake has changed his skin. But one must start from the beginning: this is essential. To bite the stone and to bark: Lord, Lord, Lord! , is to serve, weeping, a heartless woman. You must leave this to the betrayed who sigh a night, or six months, or ten years.

Life is long here.

You will beware therefore of inventing prayers. You will sing humbly with the book of the poor in spirit. And you will wait.

From the last nightly spark of your madness, the first dawn will spring up!

The crater of the heart cries and thunders and the black vomit will leave the cloud, then fall back in grey famine on the field and the vineyard. The prayer that devastates passion is like that. But when the heart has fallen asleep in the balm of the years, when the flesh has died and the blood has gone pale and when the marrow has gone dry, and when love is past and when sorrow is past, when love and sorrow and hatred have become ghosts that the sword penetrates as it does water and in which the lip hits nothing more than its own wound, as in molten glass, it is then that you speak to God no longer of yourself and of your own miserable unhappiness, but of man, and of the foam, and of the sand, and of the wind and the rain! Do you know which Saint said, Behold brother wind and sister rain?

O my son, if you knew what things man can tell God when man's flesh becomes a cry, the cry of God worshipping himself!

You do not have the face of a man who is listening, Miguel. You are thinking too much of your own sorrow. Why do you seek sorrow? Why are you afraid of losing that which has managed to find you? Penance is not sorrow. It is love.

DON MIGUEL

I hear you Father. Far be it from me the poor desire to drown my shame in the rapture of my sorrow! Let God's hands measure the bitter dosage of day and night, not mine! No: the beautiful innocent sky will not say, here is Manara bringing me a sorrow daubed in colours that he worships like the skin of a crying prostitute! No, Father: you will have in me a docile animal to turn your mill, an ox that will allow its neck and flanks to be anointed with that pity that heals the sting of the goad and puts to sleep for the night the burn of the whip. So that dawn may find us strong! And as happy as the merry crow of the cock! And full of a vigour hungry for expiation!

THE ABBOT

God's goodness! He is already chatting, my Manara, like a monk begging for his poor amidst a laughing colourful crowd, at noon on Sunday, when the Christian sun resounds, when the whole town tastes of a Mass that was too long and of Sunday lunch. Eh, slow down, sir. Spare your eloquence and fire for the autumn day and the winter night, when, barefoot, dirty, and dressed with the odour of years, you will rattle your bowl under the window of the bigot, at the door of the old greedy merchant, or in the hallway of the prostitute that is so generous as to make you cry. Eh, take your time, sir, take your time. We aren't there yet, are we? I look and see, may heaven forgive me, not the mangy donkey with a hollow back, loaded with the week's bread, not the donkey from the mill that comes to eat from the hand of the friar doorkeeper, but rather a battle-horse well-fed with barley, washed in Mauritanian sand, and spurred by the Pagan. What aflame! What a frightening impatience! Take it easy; take it easy, my dear son! And with a little goodwill everything will work out. I go at once to give the necessary orders.

He goes out

DON MIGUEL

Look at the moon, look at the earth, look at the man so weak and his great sorrow. And yet, despite all these things that are, I dare not say that You are.

Who am I then that I should dare say that You are? I am not sure, I have no right to be sure of anything apart from one: of my love, of my love, of my blind love for You. Nothing is pure, except my love for You, nothing is great, except my love for You. The dream has vanished; the passion has run away, the remembrance was cancelled. Love has remained. Nothing is sincere, except my love for You; nothing is real, except my love for You, nothing is immortal, except my love for You.

For I am nothing but one dead man among the dead whom I have loved, I am nothing but a name that fills the mouth of the living with sand. What's left is Love. Ah, Beauty!, the sad, poor Beauty! But I want to praise Beauty, for it is from it that Sorrow is born, the beloved of the Beloved. Your great love burns my heart, your great love my sole certainty. O tears! O hunger for eternity! O joy! Alas! Forgive! Alas! Love me!

FIFTH FLASH

In front of the church of Caridad, Seville. Gay Sunday crowd. Two religious men of the Order of Caridad on the fore of the scene.

FIRST RELIGIOUS MAN

So, then, what do you think, brother? As for me, I am still like the leaves of the aspen. That so simple a language should fill your head and your heart with heaven is something, in truth, that surpasses our way of understanding. I had to make a big effort, especially towards the end of the speech, to hold back my tears; and at the bottom of my throat, I still have a choked cough that stings like the nettle. What a holy man, friar Miguel of God! And what a skillful orator! I want to wait here for our reverend Father and ask him what effect such a beautiful language can have on the heart of God. I have not studied, I read with difficulty what is in the books; spade and rake are my usual companions; and it is enough for a word that's just a bit difficult to come poking my ear, and there I am as mute as our friend the earthworm. Today, instead, I understood everything; the good word of the penitent has fallen into my heart like a handful of precious seed. And do you know that at the beginning of the sermon I had to close my eyes and bite my lip so as not to laugh? Is this the way to speak of our Lord?, I thought; here is a mule-driver's or a spinster's language; and are we children to hear such things said to us? And then, suddenly, I perceived that that voice did not come from a man's mouth, but as if from the lips of a deep wound. And when he spoke to us of the Lord who walked on the sea, his eloquence became sweet to my ear as the voice of great waters suddenly calm and penetrated by a light of tenderness.

SECOND RELIGIOUS MAN

I have followed that singular speech like you, Brother, in all its points. I liked its movement and colour, but see, I have become yellow among the parchments, and my old head is that of a librarian. Alas! What strange creatures men are!

Certainly, frank speaking can be enthralling, but speaking too frankly often touches on heresy; and being carried away by passion agreeable that it may seem will never equal, in my opinion, a well-pondered order.

FIRST RELIGIOUS MAN

It's not for me, surely, to contradict you, Brother; the most boring preachers know less than you do. Grant, anyway, that the word was edifying, and that, as it came from the heart, it found the way into the heart. Consider Manara's life too, his horrible past, his ardent repentance; this love for the poor that stings him like a fire, and makes him run around from early morning, as dirty as a pig, his beard in the wind, hunger and thirst in his mouth, a bowl in his hand; this terrible humility that hits his knees like a stone twenty times a day, and throws him down, all in tears, at the feet of a beggar who teases him and on the hard road of the prostitute; this funny tenderness for the little ones, that wins for our madman, from charmed mothers, caresses like on gives to a donkey, to a cow and I too find myself at times speaking to him too sweetly, as when you discoveryou have destroyed the den of some small animal in the garden with the stroke of a spade. Consider again this bitter gratitude that for him makes all this earth of sorrow and sins a host sweet to his saliva, a comfortable kneeler; didn't I surprise him, one day, prostrated in a field, while he talked to the deaf clay as to his mother? And it was a Sunday last month didn't I see him run to a stone a drunkard had thrown at him, pick it up, and kiss it ever so tenderly?

But there he comes out of the church, surrounded by beggars. See how he talks, red-checked and breathless, with the Reverend Abbot who smiles back at him. I never saw him so joyful and childlike.

SECOND RELIGIOUS MAN

What is this?

The paralytic beggar Johannes Mendelez, all numb and stiff, pitifully drags himself out of the church. Laughter and cries welcome him into the square.

A MAN'S VOICE

Look at our crippled stoup-kisser, Johannes Mendelez, that old thief, struck by God's anger. Come here, come here everybody! We are allowed to laugh a bit after those long litanies.

A CHILD'S VOICE

Now I throw this stone into his teeth. Yesterday my dog bit him, and he called me with an affectionate voice, certainly in order to beat me.

> *The stone hits Johannes full in the chest,*
> *and he falls with a cry.*

DON MIGUEL

Lord, they have hit a poor sick old man, and I see faces of men and of Christians lit up with pleasure, as if the juggler had unfolded his carpet.

A WOMAN'S VOICE

It is Johannes Mendelez, the crippled old crow thief and lame, whom a child has hit with a stone, my good monk. It is only Johannes, the gallows-pendant, who was released last winter, after fourteen years in the galleys. It'd be better to kill him, like the old dog he is. When a bone is thrown to him, he starts praying, to tease us, and then he comes back at sunset to steal the dog's soup from honest people.

DON MIGUEL

Johannes, Johannes, do you hear me?

JOHANNES

You are the holy monk Manara. I recognize your voice. It is a sweet voice.

DON MIGUEL

Johannes, place your soul in God's hands, you look like someone who is going to die.

JOHANNES

Alas, no! The hour has not come yet. Don't you worry, good monk. Alas, no. In spite of my old age and weakness and pain, God refuses me my sleep. Ill have to live days and days, nights and nights, to crawl like a worm, screech like an axle that has not been oiled, fighting over the marrowless bone with a stray dog. The moment has not com. Expiation is long, my good monk.

DON MIGUEL

Expiation is very long, Johannes, but it is also very sweet, Johannes. And you do not speak like an enemy of God.

JOHANNES

For a very long time I was an enemy of God, like my father the bandit, and my mother the street-girl. My sad mother did not have the courage to strangle me, she fed me with her thief's milk on her prostitute's bed. I was eighth years old when a fornicating priest, moved to pity, spoke to me of the Father, of the Son, sand of the Spirit, and seeing I was weeping, wept bitterly. It was he who taught me to pray, and I've prayed for him, the bad priest, and for my miserable mother. And when the sweet time for love dame, my heart fell in love with a young gypsy, wild like me, and rejected like me. She loved me, and her people chased her away like a bitch, because of her love for a Christian bastard. The days were hard, good monk. Then I stole, to feed her sweet woman's mouth. The life of the galleys slowly ate away my bones; and when my leg were drenched like a rag under the rain they threw me ashore with a pair of crutches, and I came to die here, where God had me born.

DON MIGUEL

Lord, Lord, I call you from Capernaum.
Lord, Lord, I life my voice from the land of the
Gadarenes; Lord, Lord, I think of you at the borders of
Tyre and Sidon; Lord, Lord, my voice reaches you from
the villages of Decapolis;
Lord, Lord, I shout to you from Bethsaida;
Lord, Lord, come to my aid at the borders of Judaea
beyond the Jordan.
Amen.

To the paralytic.

You have suffered much from men, Johannes, my brother. And what name do you give God, in your thoughts? Do you call Him Sorrow, or Justice, or Vengence?

JOHANNES

I call him by the name which is his, friar Manara; that same name that you have shouted a while ago from the pulpit, good friar Manara.

DON MIGUEL

And what is it?

JOHANNES

Love.

DON MIGUEL

Throw away your crutches.

After a moment of hesitation, he throws away his crutches.

DON MIGUEL

Get up and walk.

Johannes Mendelez gets u and without looking at anyone goes back towards the church shouting with a terrible voice: Hosanna hosanna! The abbot of the Caridad and his monks kiss the dress of Don Miguel Manara. The people shout: Miracle! And throw themselves to their knees imploring the blessing of the Penitent.

SIXTH FLASH

A courtyard of the convent of Caridad. The silence of the last moments of night. The sky is full of stars, and yet it seems that day is already there. A small door opens noiselessly. Miguel Manara appears, a lantern in his hand and a shoulder-bag on his shoulder. He is very old; his hair is white, his hands tremble. He leans on a stick.

DON MIGUEL

O my heart! O my child! You did not sleep, and here is the day. Here is the day, it arrives and it is astonished at finding yesterday's moon in the sky. Here are you alone under the cold tears of a night lost forever, alone with your thoughts of yesterday, like the mowed grass. O face in tears! O severe Eternity!

Silence

They are dead. Unknown sleepers surround me. Those whom my heart loved have been dead a long time. Only one saw me growing old: the friar gardener, the one who knows the thought of the herbs and the intentions of the air. All the others are dead. O morning moon! O sad look of Eternity.

Silence

Not everything has been said, not everything has been done. One has to pray, one has to act. The immense heart of anguish is like the noise of the wing that is broken on water. The whole night, the whole night! Anguish was at my side like a wife who loves and whom for a long time one has stopped loving.

Silence

I got up earlier and I have joined these strong hands in the glow of the lantern. I have much to do today, and my heart is right in loving the weak lamp of the morning and the mechanical prayer in the empty blue cold, which does not fall from the moon and is not the breath of the morning.

Silence

O morning moon! How you have the face of those who see strange and profound things! The hungry man bites his own breath and eats it, and falls asleep in the water of his own weakness. The sick worker collects his tools coughing. The abandoned girl recognizes with fright the garret, the splinter of mirror and the broom: she blankly watches her barren womb, and suddenly thinks of the shrieking of the well.

Silence

Lord, Lord, give us our daily hope! O Father, O Son, give us our daily courage! As the leper beggar, his back stuck to the wall, stretches his bowl towards the soup, so will I stretch my young heart towards the perfumed warmth of the amorous life!

Give me my daily share of love, and measure it out generously, because of other: so that I may go, surfeited, towards those who do not love you and insult me; so that I may say: this is his liberality. For these are not the gifts of his heart, but only the crumbs swept away from his table; and here is what remains in the bowl of the unworthy and surfeited servant.

O road! O city! O kingdom! O earth! Come and eat! For thus is the Most High, for He is the Lord Love! I am Manara, the one who lies when he says: I love. And because I said to the Eternal that I loved Him, my heart is joyful and my hands are as desirable as bread.

What does Paul, the scoundrel, say, and what does Mary, the prostitute, say? What has been stolen and lost was stolen and lost.

I am Mañara. And the one I love says: these things have not been. If he has stolen, if he has killed: let these things not have been! Only he is.

Silence. Dawn at the horizon.

The silence has the smell of the apple-tree that dreams, the air wears it angel's robe. The breath of the earth is like the yawning of the ox. The great wall takes the colour of the almond-tree. Here is dawn. The well creaks like the lazy schoolboy. The echo gets up from its bed. Here are the water carriers. The straw of the stables shakes. The cock, the cock crows as to make man's heart weep. Here is day! O earth! O beloved!

He puts out the lantern, then he listens intently

And I hear a bell: one two three four five! A monk's hour. And I hear the trumpet: Tra ra! Tra ra ra! A soldier's hour.

He goes towards the door on the street,
but suddenly on the threshold,
a form wrapped in a dark mantle stands up.

THE UNKNOWN ONE

Stop.

DON MIGUEL

I do not know this man and the door is locked. He could not have climbed over the wall.

THE UNKNOWN ONE

You got up earlier than usual, Mañara, you have lit the small lamp and you have been praying. And now you want to take up your work for the last time.

DON MIGUEL

Certainly I am day-dreaming. Yet I recognize the voice and remember the words. It was a long, long time ago. Where then did I hear this? But I'm wasting my time. Come on then, old heart, courage! And you, old legs, come on!

THE UNKNOWN ONE

Stop.

The game has gone on too long. Everything has done its time. We shall no longer go to take bread to those children, that new bowl to Pablo Perez, our handsome blind fiddler. Everything has done its time, Mañara. There is a time for youth; there is time for old age. Then comes death. Thus speaks the Spirit of the Earth.

DON MIGUEL

A veil is fluttering before my eyes, my legs are sinking in sand, my stomach is closing, anguish is catching my throat.

THE SPIRIT

I am the Spirit of the Earth. Beware. You have a ghost's name on your lips. I am, I am. Truly I am, Through the heart and the reason of Man. Look at me. I have put on my true form. Here is the Lord; here is the Prince of the kingdoms of the earth. Recognize me.

He opens his mantle.

DON MIGUEL

O terrible face! O sad face...

THE SPIRIT

I am the one who is. I am the heart of the earth. All the rest is vanity. As the handsome thief clasps the excited prostitute in his arms, so I hold the warm earth tight against my breast.

Listen how the earth, the wide-wombed girl, teases you, ghost-hunters, empty toys of Justice. Listen, listen to what the great lover whispers in your hairy ear: "What do they know of me, these gelded ones? I make them pay dearly the joy of my odour! You, you are my lover and my master! Injustice drugs your mouth, your hairy hand is warm on my head. I will bring handsome royal sons for you, who will love the mysterious gold and the vapour of blood. I will give them a forehead as low as yours, my love, and enormous hands, and large licking mouths, my love; and their faces will be warm and pale like the lightning. And from the first day they will seek their joy in the grief of little ones".

Thus speaks the Earth to its Lord, to its Master:

"We shall make for our daughter a bed of scarlet and her two breasts will call the passer-by like the fountains of the city, like the unsealed springs. And our daughter will be as beautiful as the pomegranate broken by the weight of its own fall. And she will say with a milky stammer: love cannot be a sin. And behold! Your royal seal will be transparent on her face long kissed by the fire that passes and forgets. Her tongue will then be like the head of the snake that dances and the shadow of the joyful hours will be encrusted on the dial of her face. And one cay her face will be like a dance and the shadow of the joyful hours will be your mantle and you will give her children. "

Thus speaks the Earth to its Lord, to its Master:

"The sons will be clothed in iron, the daughters will shine with perfumes. And gold will resound on the tables. And the wombs will offer themselves to whoever offers most. Whoever has a sweet heart and will meet my eyes will be like the frightened insect in the wound of the earth. He will look at his mother and will say: I smell betrayal, why isn't that the face of an old woman that barks at the moon? And he will be sleepy and will not dare entrust his head to his wife's breast: for adultery will have passed there. And they'll have time to laugh over it! The adulterous man dreams poisonous dreams! And the man will call on his daughter, the virgin, and glancing at her mouth he will bow his head."

Thus speaks the Earth to its Lord, to its Master:

"And man will entrust his heritage to the worms of the ruins, to the nettle's root, in a place which his fiery-eyed brother does not visit. And all mouths will be full of lies, and all hearts will secretly desire death. The strongest and greediest of our sons will be king and the weakest and the most cunning will be priest, and they will hold hands and laugh in their beards. And on the Mount of Temptation, once a year, you will blow on the secret fire through the rumbling of the crater, and what is supposed to swim will walk like the beast of the forest and what is supposed to crawl will fly like fire. And the vermin of the great wall will come and reveal to us the secret thought of man."

Thus speaks the Earth, to the prince of the Kingdoms of the Earth:

"Come on, Manara, get up, you know very well that you belong to me. Did you not give me the best of yourself, the poem of your youth?"

DON MIGUEL

Lifting his hands to heaven

I am a stranger on the earth; do not hide your commands from me.

Do not leave me alone in my distress, come close; there is none else to help.

My soul lies in the dust; give me life according to your word.

Teach me discernment and knowledge, for I trust in your commands.

Listen them to my cry, for I am in the depths of distress.

Bring my soul out of this prison.

The apparition vanishes.

THE SPIRIT OF HEAVEN

Miguel! Miguel!

DON MIGUEL

Here I am.

A very long silence. A lizard comes to warm itself on a stone near the dead man. The small door of the Convent opens slowly. Enter the friar gardener – he is the first religious man of the Fifth Flash. He is extremely old and broke. He walks in very short steps looking at the ground. Reaching the corpse of Miguel, he stops, showing no surprise.

THE FRIAR GARDENER

Friar Miguel, are you sleeping?

He touches him lightly. Silence. He recites a short prayer and makes a large sign of the cross embracing the four horizons

Now I am alone.

Now I am among the living like the naked branch whose dry noise frightens the evening wind. But my heart is joyful like the nest that remembers and like the earth that hopes under the snow. For I know that everything is where it is supposed to be and goes where it is supposed to go: to the place assigned to it by a Wisdom that - heaven be praised – is not our own

He considers at length the calm face of Miguel.

Here is your brother, Magdalene.

Here is brother, Teresa.

TO THE PRAISE OF CHRIST. AMEN.

CPSIA information can be obtained
at www.ICGtesting.com
Printed in the USA
FFOW03n1744150317
33496FF